WRITTEN BY

Race Day

Copyright © CWR 2012
Published 2012 by CWR, Waverley Abbey House, Waverley Lane, Farnham,
Surrey GU9 8EP, UK
Tel: 01252 784700 Email: mail@cwr.org.uk Registered Charity No. 294387
Registered Limited Company No. 1990308
Front cover image: Getty Images/Vetta/Andrew Rich
Concept development, editing, design and production by CWR.
Printed in England by Linney Print.
All rights reserved. No part of this publication may be reproduced, stored in
a retrieval system, or transmitted, in any form or by any means, electronic,
mechanical, photocopying, recording or otherwise, without the prior
permission in writing of CWR.
Unless otherwise indicated, all Scripture references are from The Holy Bible,
New International Version (Anglicised edition), copyright © 1979, 1984,
2011 by Biblica (formerly International Bible Society).
Message: Scripture taken from THE MESSAGE. Copyright © 1993, 1994, 1995,
1996, 2000, 2001, 2002. Used by permission of NavPress Publishing Group.
ESV: Scripture quotations are from The Holy Bible, English Standard Version,
published by HarperCollins Publishers © 2001 by Crossway Bibles, a division
of Good News Publishers. Used by permission. All rights reserved.

HOW TO GET THE BEST OUT OF *LIFE EVERY DAY*

HERE ARE A FEW SUGGESTIONS:

- Ideally, carve out a regular time and place each day, with as few distractions as possible. Ask God what He has to say to you.

- Read the Bible passages suggested in the 'Big Picture' references. (As tempting as it is, try not to skip the Bible reading and get straight into the notes.)

- The 'Focus' reference then gives you one or two verses to look at in more detail. Consider what the reading is saying to you and what challenges that may bring.

- Each day's comments are part of an overall theme. Try to recall what you read the previous day so that you maintain a sense of continuity.

- Spend time thinking about how to apply what God has said to you. Ask Him to help you do this.

- Pray the prayer at the end as if it were your own. Perhaps add your own prayer in response to what you have read and been thinking about.

Join in the conversation on Facebook
www.facebook.com/jefflucasuk

TUES 01 JAN

The race worth running in

BIG PICTURE
2 Timothy 4:1–8
Philippians 3:1–10

FOCUS:
'I have fought the good fight, I have finished the race.' (2 Tim. 4:7)

MOST of us are runners. Jumping out of bed in the morning, our first action of the day is like that of an athlete staring up at a scoreboard – we peer at the clock. From our first waking second, we hop onto a treadmill of activity, bustling through our days at breakneck speed. Our running isn't just about the rate at which we hurtle through life, but in the priorities that we set. We chase after goals of achievement and accumulation, and insist that we haven't got time to engage in 'unproductive' activities like strolls in the park, long evenings of giggling chatter with vintage friends, bedtime games with children or grandchildren, or the luxury of a long bath and a book. We're runners.

Eugene Peterson, capturing the passion of Paul in his writing to Timothy, has the veteran athlete/apostle declare, 'This is the only race worth running.' As we'll see, this is a theme that Paul repeats. Participating in the Christian marathon is a priceless privilege and has eternal consequences. It's a trek, run with Jesus going ahead as our example and yet alongside us with His daily presence; a race with a stadium full of forerunners whose own stories of perseverance and faith show us that we're in a noble line. Compared with this, Paul considered everything as garbage (Phil. 3:8). It's race day, and our turn has come. Right at the beginning of our journey in this theme, let's affirm that even when the going is tough, and the track suddenly banks into an unexpected uphill climb, the journey we take is truly the only one worth taking.

Prayer: Lord, help me to run, not after that which doesn't matter or count, but to run as a winner in Your eyes. Amen.

… the journey we take is truly the only one worth taking

WED 02 JAN

Resolutions

BIG PICTURE
Acts 20:13–38
2 Timothy 4:1–8

FOCUS:
'I consider my life worth nothing to me; my only aim is to finish the race and complete the task the Lord Jesus has given me … testifying to the good news of God's grace.'
(Acts 20:24)

IT'S the season for resolutions. Many of us have resolved to eat less, exercise more, shed bad habits and embrace healthy disciplines. Some scoff at the idea of resolutions, insisting that the proverbial leopard can never change its spots. I'm sad for anyone who does not believe in the possibility of change.

And yet hopeless resignation is often found among God's people. Despite our teachings that God is at work in us in daily transformation, many of us live with a subconscious conviction that ultimately we're destined to fail spectacularly. Speaking at a men's retreat recently, I asked how many of the Christian men present wrestled with the idea that, for them, some moral disaster was not only likely but inevitable. Many of the attendees – and remember that these were the keen ones who were giving up their Saturdays to study Scripture with me – confessed that this was their fear.

Yesterday we heard Paul speaking to Timothy about what one writer calls the 'beautiful fight'. He was able to say that he had held on to faith through the marathon – but this was a retrospective statement. Some years earlier, Paul had addressed the elders at Ephesus – the church where Timothy was now in leadership – and had stated his ambition to run hard and well to the finish line. And now, he is able to look back and see that ambition fulfilled.

Want to run well in the race, all the way? You can. Finishing badly is not inevitable; on the contrary. Believe it, and then today reaffirm your resolution to be a winner, for and with Christ.

Finishing badly is not inevitable …

Prayer: Help me to be hopeful and ambitious by Your grace, Lord – that I might run and finish the race as a winner, for Your glory. Amen.

THURS 03 JAN

Hold tight to faith

BIG PICTURE
2 Timothy 4:1–8
Luke 22:31–38

FOCUS:
'I have kept the faith.'
(2 Tim. 4:7)

PERHAPS the most important race in the modern Olympics is the 100 metre sprint; certainly it gains the most attention. But the climax to the games in ancient times was the relay race, where teams of competitors combined their skills and energies as they raced in turn to the finish post. In the relay, the handover of the baton is the vital moment. With perfect timing the baton is passed, and the receiver takes hold of it with a firm grip. Dropping the baton means disaster and loss.

As Paul talks about 'keeping the faith', the baton imagery is helpful. The words he uses here are similar to when he talks about 'laying hands' on people in recognition for ministry (1 Tim. 5:22), an act of solemnity and decisiveness. Paul grabbed faith and held on tight. Again I turn to Peterson: 'I've run hard right to the finish, believed all the way' (2 Tim. 4:7).

Some days I don't exactly lose my faith, I just mislay it. I find myself in situations where tiredness, cynicism or fear mean that I stagger through a day – or a season – hoping to survive, rather than exercising faith in persistent prayer. I place myself in the position of not receiving because I'm not asking for anything. I drop the baton. Like Peter, I'm sifted and shaken, my faith the primary target in the spiritual war.

Perhaps that's where you are right now. Instead of moving down the track, you're parked on the side, wincing because of injury, sad because of failure. Get up. Take hold of the baton. Believing all the way means believing today.

Prayer: **Lord, help me to find faith where I have been faithless, and to hold on to and keep the faith today. Amen.**

FRI 04 JAN

Relevant

BIG PICTURE
1 Corinthians
9:24–27
Matthew 18:2–5

FOCUS:
'Everyone who competes in the games goes into strict training.'
(1 Cor. 9:25)

WORRIED that his friends in Corinth were becoming spiritually flabby, Paul sought to stir them to focus, action and discipline. And so he used a metaphor that immediately grabbed the attention of the Christians in Corinth, as he talks first about a running race – and then switches the metaphor over to boxing. The Corinthians would have understood what he meant immediately, because their city was a sports capital of the day. The Isthmian games, the forerunner to the Olympics, were held in Corinth every other year. The streets of the city would have teemed with athletes and trainers, all hoping for success in their chosen sport. But they were more than hopeful. Every day the citizens of Corinth would have seen the grimacing faces and sweating bodies of athletes dedicated to their chosen sport. They were in the games, but not playing games; the Isthmian event was about passion, not amusement.

Before we continue our journey, let's pause and see that Paul used a contemporary, relevant illustration in order to stir the Corinthian believers out of their lethargy. Paul's use of the sporting metaphor shows that we need inspirational and applicable preaching and teaching that will connect our Sunday mornings to our Monday mornings. Like Paul, Jesus used everyday events to illustrate His teaching, drawn from the lives of His hearers. Pray for those who are responsible for teaching and preaching in our churches, that their communications will be rooted in eternal truth – illustrated and applied for today.

> They were in the games, but not playing games …

Prayer: Lord, I pray for those with the huge responsibility of bringing relevant and applicable teaching in the Church. Amen.

CWR MINISTRY EVENTS

Please pray for the team

Date	Event	Place	Presenter(s)
Jan – Mar	Developing Pastoral Care (Christian Vocation) (six Thursdays)	Waverley Abbey House	Andy Peck, Philip Greenslade and Lynn Penson
Jan	Counselling Training Enquirers' Morning	WAH	Counselling Training Team
Jan	Insight into Assertiveness	WAH	Chris Ledger
Jan	Transformed by the Presence of Jesus	WAH	Liz Babbs
8-31 Jan	Marriage on Track (for the Salvation Army)	WAH	Andrew & Lynn Penson
Feb	Bible Text to Engaging Sermon	WAH	Andy Peck
–17 Feb	Bible Discovery Weekend	WAH	Philip Greenslade
Feb	Insight into Bullying	WAH	Helena Wilkinson
0-21 Feb	Managing Conflict	WAH	Hilary Turner and Liz Moles
Feb	Christ Empowered Living	Pilgrim Hall	Mick & Lynette Brooks

lease also pray for students and tutors on our ongoing **BA in Counselling** rogramme at Waverley and Pilgrim Hall and our **Certificate and Diploma of hristian Counselling** and **MA in Integrative Psychotherapy** held at London chool of Theology.

For further details and a full list of CWR's courses, phone +44 (0)1252 784719 or visit the CWR website at www.cwr.org.uk Pilgrim Hall: www.pilgrimhall.com

www.cwr.org.uk

WEEKEND

05/06 JAN

1 Corinthians 9:24 // 1 Corinthians 3:1–15

What the prize is not

The gold medal is the coveted prize that Olympians pursue. The thought that they might bring home the gold inspires them to discipline and dedication.

As Paul encourages the Corinthians to pursue a prize, it's vital that we understand what that prize is. We do not run to pursue salvation; it is not awarded because of our efforts, disciplines or accomplishments. Forgiveness and eternal life are a free gift to all in Christ, because of the final victory of Jesus. The cross secures our pardon. Grace is given freely, not won by our performance.

If we don't get this truth established in our hearts and minds, then our lives will be blighted by fear and insecurity. I've met plenty of Christians with troubled hearts and furrowed brows who intellectually believe that they are saved by grace, but emotionally seem to believe that they are saved by works. Earlier in his letter to the Corinthians, Paul speaks of our works for Christ – but doesn't suggest that works lead to salvation. Paul wasn't concerned about losing his *salvation*, but his *reward*. They are quite distinct.

We do not run to pursue salvation …

To ponder: Why do we often slip into thinking that our salvation is something we work for, rather than a free gift?

MON 07 JAN

Fully obtain

BIG PICTURE
1 Corinthians 9:24
2 Thessalonians 2:13–17

FOCUS:
'Run in such a way as to get the prize.'
(1 Cor. 9:24)

IT WAS 44 years in the waiting, and produced one of the most exciting football matches I have ever seen. Manchester City were playing Queens Park Rangers, and needed to secure a win lest their rivals, Manchester United, took the Premier League Championship. Feelings were running high. All looked lost, with City a goal behind and just about 120 seconds of time left to play, when suddenly, one brilliant goal was followed by another. I've never seen such scenes of exuberance. The only comparable event was the 1966 World Cup win for England. City deserved to win, because they went absolutely all out, despite being in the exhausting final moments of a hard game.

As Paul talks about 'getting' the prize, he uses a Greek word that means 'fully obtain'. Just as the City players refused to give up until the final whistle, and snatched victory from defeat, so we are called to give 100% of ourselves to Christ each day. But even as I write that, I'm not sure what it actually means. Often I hear preachers challenge congregations with the question, 'Does Jesus have all of you?', but I do not know how to answer honestly. I believe in total surrender, and want that to be my experience, but how can I honestly measure if it is true of me? All I can do is make myself fully available to Him today, determined to obey what He says, and resolve that, if He calls, I'm ready to respond. We saw earlier that Paul ran with a firm grip on faith; those who 'lay hold' of faith will 'lay hold' of prizes.

Prayer: Whatever today brings, I offer myself in unreserved surrender to You, Lord, to live in the fullness of Your purposes. Amen.

TUES 08 JAN

Towards the prize

BIG PICTURE
Philippians 3:1–14
1 Corinthians 9:24

FOCUS:
'I press on towards the goal to win the prize for which God has called me heavenwards in Christ Jesus.' (Phil. 3:14)

TODAY we turn momentarily to another reference to prize winning, where Paul writes to the Philippians. Understanding the background of his metaphor might be useful. The runners in the ancient stadia ran towards a goal marker, a pillar which marked the finishing line – hence Paul's talk of running towards the *goal* for the prize. And there were other markers on the starting line and then half way down the track, each inscribed with a word chosen to spur the athletes on to victory. The starting post had the word *excel* written on it; a call to be way above the average, and to refuse mediocrity. The second pillar said *hasten*: perhaps, just when runners' bodies were starting to protest and slacken, a reminder to redouble their efforts and accelerate towards the finish. The third said *turn*, because the runners would have to race around that pillar and sprint back to the starting point.

Paul gets so excited about using the metaphor of the prize that he doesn't explain it fully to the Philippians, and so there are a variety of suggestions about what he means. One suggestion is that, just as athletes were 'called up' by the panel of overseeing judges to hear their name, their father's name and their country of birth announced by heralds before being awarded the prize, so Paul is referring to being called 'heavenwards' to receive the 'well done' from Jesus. It's difficult to think in these terms when life right now might be tough, but let's ask God to give us a sense of eternal perspective, wherever we might find ourselves on the track.

Prayer: Lord, help me to excel and to hasten as I run the race in Your strength. Amen.

… let's ask God to give us a sense of eternal perspective …

WED 09 JAN

All over bar the shouting

BIG PICTURE
Philippians 3:14
Romans 15:1–6

FOCUS:
'I press on towards the goal to win the prize for which God has called me heavenwards in Christ Jesus.' (Phil. 3:14)

THE idea of Paul's 'prize' being the incredible moment of being 'called up on high' to receive congratulation and rewards from God Himself demands some further thought – and should prompt us to worship.

If I'm honest, for all of the writing and speaking on grace and God's love that I do, I still live with a subconscious notion that God the perfect One can never be really pleased or even delighted with my efforts. I am all too aware that my very best intentions are inevitably flawed with mixed motives and inconsistency. My purity is too often punctuated by sin, and I feel like I did when I presented my course work for GCSE Art many years ago in school. My art teacher made it very obvious that he didn't like me and was disappointed with my work, and so for just one week I trebled my efforts and did my best. I won't forget the report card he filled in: 'Jeff gets an A+ – for one week of work only. After that he lapsed back into being uncreative, lazy and inattentive – the usual routine when it comes to Jeff and art.' As you can imagine, I wasn't motivated by his sarcasm and caustic tone, although I admit I wasn't the best pupil.

Sometimes God can seem like that art teacher: only ever pleased with us, at best, for a moment or two. But that's not Paul's vision of Jesus. Paul is running to win because of the delight of meeting face to face with the wonderful One who gives endurance and encouragement. Eugene Peterson again on 2 Timothy 4:7: 'All that's left now is the shouting – God's applause!'

Prayer: **Thank You for the truth about Your character Lord; full of grace and encouragement. Your mercy inspires me to press onward. Amen.**

THURS 10 JAN

Run in such a way

BIG PICTURE
1 Corinthians 9:24
Galatians 2:1–5

FOCUS:
'Run in such a way as to get the prize.'
(1 Cor. 9:24)

MY SON-IN-LAW, Ben, is experimenting with a new way of running, using some shoes that, unlike traditional running shoes, have no support at all, and fit around the feet like a skin. The effect is more like running barefoot. He is working on running on his toes, rather than his heels. Apparently the traditional way can cause shock to the limbs, and heel-running means that you are always braking, whereas toe-running propels you forward. There's a right and a wrong way to run.

I'm always delighted when someone becomes a Christian. But I get a little nervous too, as I wonder about what kind of Christian they are going to become. And I'm not talking about them being half-hearted, uncommitted, or drifting away from faith. I've discovered that it's possible to be a zealous, white-hot Christian, who is hurtful, damaging and brings discredit to God. Our tone can be harsh, we can be over-preoccupied with single issues, impatient with other Christians who don't share the same burdens and passions that we have.

Working hard at being a Christian, being disciplined, diligent, attentive and faithful, doesn't mean that we are going to be spiritually healthy. As Paul says 'run in such a way as to win', we're reminded that running takes huge effort and energy – but it's possible to put all that effort in, and still run a losing race. Here our friends can help us – are we open to their correction, can they nudge us back on track? Running isn't enough: running like a winner is called for.

Prayer: Teach me how to run well, and to run as a winner, Lord. Amen.

There's a right and a wrong way to run

FRI 11 JAN

Temperance

BIG PICTURE
1 Corinthians 9:25
1 Timothy 6:11–21

FOCUS:
'Everyone who competes in the games goes into strict training.'
(1 Cor. 9:25)

WE'LL return later to the themes of winning and prizes. In the meantime, let's look at a word that isn't heard too often these days: temperance. It evokes images of poker-faced Victorians, berating society on the evils of self-indulgence, railing against fun as well as excess. In his exhortation to the Corinthians, Paul uses a word that is translated 'strict training' – it is actually the word 'temperate', and it only occurs in 1 Corinthians. It refers to the ten months of preparatory training (and workouts in the gymnasium immediately before the games) under the direction of judges who had themselves been instructed for ten months in their role. There was nothing casual about these games. Everyone involved followed a careful plan in order to perform at their maximum potential.

Epictetus, a Greek philosopher, offered this advice to the would-be winners: 'Thou must be orderly, living on spare food; abstain from confections; make a point of exercising at the appointed time, in heat and in cold.'

Horace (a Roman poet) describes the price that the athlete has to pay: 'The youth who would win in the race hath borne and done much, he hath sweat and hath been cold: he hath abstained from love and wine.'

Before we begin to talk about discipline specifically, we should know that Christianity calls for single-minded dedication and commitment. Just as athletes often say that their sport is about 99% drudgery (as they prepare) and 1% excitement (as they perform), so we are not called to constant exhilaration, but to a faithful daily run.

Prayer: Lord, when it seems futile for me to run the race, then help me to do so on that day. Amen.

12/13 JAN

Colossians 2:1–5 // Titus 1:5–8

Negative connotations

We saw yesterday that 'temperance' is not a popular word – and 'discipline' has also been overlaid with negative connotations. It conjures up images of parents punishing a child. But as we will see, discipline is actually a way to freedom, not a method of punishing the lawless.

Some Christians make discipline an end in itself; so the exertions of the disciplines themselves become the aim. The dedicated runner covers six miles a day, and after a while, that is his aim. He forgets the cardio-vascular benefits, or the bonus of being more alert and efficient because of taking time to exercise. Something similar can happen to Christians. We pray because good Christians pray, we read the Bible, not to have our vision expanded, or because we want to take on board truth, but because that's what good Christians are supposed to do. We feel better because we have ticked the boxes of our pious habits, but forget the purpose *behind* those habits.

Paul didn't think that way at all, but saw discipline as a means to an end. He wants to run well in the race of life, so he embraces the means to do so.

… discipline as a means to an end

To ponder: Do you have a negative view of discipline? What would you say to someone who reacts against it by insisting that we are 'free in Christ'?

MON 14 JAN

What discipline is not: a quick fix

BIG PICTURE
2 Corinthians 3:7–18
Romans 8:29

FOCUS:
'And we all, who with unveiled faces contemplate the Lord's glory, are being transformed into his image with ever-increasing glory, which comes from the Lord … the Spirit.' (2 Cor. 3:18)

NOTICING that I had gained a few pounds recently, I consulted an expert. Without needing to go on a full-on diet, but wanting to get into better shape, I expected a step-by-step plan that would transform me from slight flabbiness to Adonis-like perfection in eight weeks …

His response surprised me. Instead of a step-by-step plan, he gave me strategies to follow each day, flexible responses that I could make when travelling, or jet-lagged, or eating out or as a guest, when it's difficult to refuse the carefully prepared (but unhealthy) meal set before you. The gym of spiritual discipline is life itself. We might give ourselves to seasons of prayer and fasting, but there is no 'quick fix' programme to spiritual maturity. Rather, we are called to establish daily patterns that will cause us to grow as we do everyday life.

God is committed to our transformation as we cooperate with Him. Transformed disciples don't have to panic when faced with a moral dilemma, and ask, 'What would Jesus do?' Instead, they know that Jesus is making them more Christlike, so that they are 'being conformed to His image' and they instinctively respond well when faced with fierce temptation. Jesus Himself didn't have to scrabble around for some biblical quotes when He was tempted in the wilderness. His habit of immersing Himself in Scripture meant that He was prepared, both in terms of what He knew and who He was. He used Scripture as a weapon, not to consult in some panicked way to find out what He should do.

Prayer: Lord, today, I freely choose to walk in Your ways; transform me by the work of Your Spirit, as I gladly submit myself to You. Amen.

TUES 15 JAN

Spiritual disciplines are not just 'spiritual'

BIG PICTURE
Colossians 3:1–17
1 Corinthians 10:23–11:1

FOCUS:
'And whatever you do, whether in word or deed, do it all in the name of the Lord Jesus, giving thanks to God the Father through him.' (Col. 3:17)

HE WAS rather good at prayer, rising before the sun to spend at least an hour in intercession. He knew the Bible like the back of his hand, and was able to fire scriptures like a gunfighter, quick on the draw. And he treated worship like a connoisseur of fine wine. If the right mix of songs and hymns were not included, he would wrinkle his nose in disgust. But he was also to navigate his way through a messy divorce, his wife no longer able to bear his pious complaining, his children terribly damaged by their father's relentless pickiness which he defended as being 'in pursuit of the best for them'. His mistake? He had divided his life into boxes, categorising what was 'spiritual' and what was not, and became proficient in performing religious duties, but careless about everyday relationships.

Metropolitan Anthony, former head of the Russian Church of Great Britain and Ireland, famously said, 'We need a spiritual reality that operates at the level of the kitchen sink.' As Paul compared spiritual development with physical training, he was not trying to create a false dualism, where prayer matters and exercise doesn't. Instead, he was saying it is useless to have a perfectly toned body, if we are not fully developed human beings, with everything we do integrated into our spiritual lives. Whatever we do, let's do it in the name of Jesus, or as Rabbi Jose, AD 100, said, 'Let all thy deeds be done for the sake of Heaven.'[1]

And if we can't do something in the name of Jesus, should we do it at all?

Prayer: Lord, save me from the temptation to separate my life into secular and sacred boxes. May all that I am be pleasing to You. Amen.

1. P.T. O'Brien, *Word Biblical Commentary Vol. 44: Colossians–Philemon* (Dallas: Word Incorporated, 2002) p.211.

WED 16 JAN

Not a straight-jacket

BIG PICTURE
2 Timothy 1:1–7
Luke 11:37–46

FOCUS:
'For the Spirit God gave us does not make us timid, but gives us power, love and self-discipline.'
(2 Tim. 1:7)

IT'S been a negative by-product of my running regime, which I've tried to follow for the last seven years. When I don't run, I feel guilty. Even when nursing a minor injury, and advised to rest, I feel bad for not running, and worse if I see a runner out on the road.

One of the reasons that some of us avoid spiritual disciplines is because we don't need any more fuel for guilt. We feel deficient enough about our Christian lives already, without adding another layer of demands that can set us up for failure. Popular author John Ortberg confessed that his initial reaction to teaching on becoming disciplined was negative: 'My immediate response was, I already feel guilty about not praying and reading the Bible enough – the last thing in the world I want is ten other things to feel guilty about not doing.'[1] Ortberg moved on from this negative view – but many of us can echo his feelings. Richard Foster, a primary voice calling for restoration of spiritual disciplines, points out that we can so easily turn chosen patterns of life into onerous demands that tower over us: 'Spiritual disciplines are intended for our good – it is possible to turn them into another set of soul killing laws.'[2]

Let's establish good *patterns* for our lives, in terms of exercise, prayer, hospitality, giving, silence, service, celebration and study, to name but a few. But these must be patterns, and not rigid train lines, lest we end up labouring under a terrible burden. A wrong attitude towards discipline means that we are placing the burden upon ourselves.

Prayer: Show me the way to embrace discipline that does not distil into legalism, loving God. Amen.

1. John Ortberg, *The Life You've Always Wanted* (Grand Rapids: Zondervan, 2002).

2. Richard J. Foster, *Celebration of Discipline: The Path to Spiritual Growth* Revised Edition (New York: HarperSanFrancisco, 1988) pp.62–76.

Let's establish good *patterns* for our lives ...

THURS 17 JAN

Saving ourselves

BIG PICTURE
Zechariah 4:1–6
John 15:1–5

FOCUS:
'So he said to me, "This is the word of the LORD to Zerubbabel: 'Not by might nor by power, but by my Spirit,' says the LORD Almighty."'
(Zech. 4:6)

TAKING a trip on a catamaran recently, I chatted with the captain about our fuel consumption. It turns out that, in four days on the water, we used around £100 of diesel. The engine was used to get us into harbour and out again, and once, for 20 minutes, when we were suddenly becalmed and needed to get going. One night, at the dockside, I was talking with the owner of a larger boat that had made a four-day trip like ours. His fuel bill was no less than £60,000. I know which I'd prefer! He had a boat that could only be propelled by fuel: ours was able to harness the freely available force of the wind: all we had to do was to hoist the sails.

That is what discipline does for us. Spiritual disciplines do not propel us in their own right, but simply position us so that God's Spirit can blow in and through us. The disciples had to wait in the upper room, so that they could be filled with the fire and wind of the Holy Spirit. Zechariah lived at a time when Jerusalem was in ruins; God reminded him that only by the power of God could the ruinous city be glorious again. It is not just that prayer changes things; it is that prayer not only changes us, even as we pray, but also brings us in quietness and with requests to the God of all power. Solitude, reflection, study and meditation do not make God speak: they help us to position ourselves to listen. We do not save ourselves through our disciplines, but our disciplines enable us to walk with the Jesus who has saved us.

> We do not save ourselves through our disciplines …

Prayer: Breathe Your life in and through me, Holy Spirit; show me how to set the sails of my life to the wind today. Amen.

FRI 18 JAN

Prayer warriors and other unhelpful labels

BIG PICTURE
Judges 6:1–16
Romans 12:3–8

FOCUS:
"'Pardon me, my lord,' Gideon replied, 'but how can I save Israel? My clan is the weakest in Manasseh, and I am the least in my family.'" (Judg. 6:15)

IT'S a phrase that always makes me feel very intimidated: just the use of those two words, prayer warriors, ushers me into instant condemnation; knowing my struggles to focus, remain awake, be creative and stay faithful in prayer, I'm tempted to give up and reserve prayer time for 999 situations (911 for our American readers!). Most Christians seem to swing between two extremes when it comes to healthily appraising themselves. Some of us think of ourselves too highly: ignoring our weaknesses, we become preoccupied with what we're good at and, like Peter, think that we'd be the last to let the Lord Jesus down. We need to experience some failure, just to put our feet on the ground, and give us a more sober assessment of our frailties.

But there's another extreme – where we look at ourselves and see nothing but weakness and lack, just like Gideon. It's this extreme that is most dangerous when it comes to embracing spiritual disciplines. Some of us dismiss ourselves from the race before we've even got down on the track, feeling that a disciplined life is for people who are a different breed from us, spiritual super saints, an elite in commitment and dedication. Surely, we insist, a life of reflection where we choose moments or seasons of silence is for those who have retreated from the world into a traditional monastic setting. But we're quite wrong. Choosing a disciplined life, and asking God to help us to stay faithful and attentive as we navigate through ordinary days, is an option available to all of us.

Prayer: Lord, save me from stopping myself fulfilling all my potential. May I understand both what I cannot do and what I can. Amen.

THE STORMBREAKER — O

CWR has recently produced *The Stormbreaker*, a brand-new DVD resource for use by individuals and small groups. Presented by Mick Brooks, the teaching is based on an issue of *Every Day with Jesus* and looks at the three days from the crucifixion to the resurrection, the time of Jesus' greatest 'storm'.

Five approximately fifteen-minute video sessions using green screen techniques, animations and relevant library footage show Mick 'appearing' in the midst of a storm, at the scene of the crucifixion and on a battlefield, resulting in a presentation guaranteed to hold the viewer's attention.

There is also an accompanying booklet containing discussion starters, prayers and Bible-reading notes from the original issue of *Every Day with Jesus*.

The foundational truths in this DVD can be explored at any time of year, but are perhaps most poignant during the Lent and Easter period. Why not consider buying this resource for a special Lent group? You will be able to study with others some of the themes which centre on the cross and the resurrection of Jesus, and find there all that is needed to face the storms of life.

The Stormbreaker
Presented by Mick Brooks
EAN: 5027957001411
£14.99 incl VAT (includes one booklet)

Additional booklets:
ISBN: 978-1-85345-838-5
£3.50 each

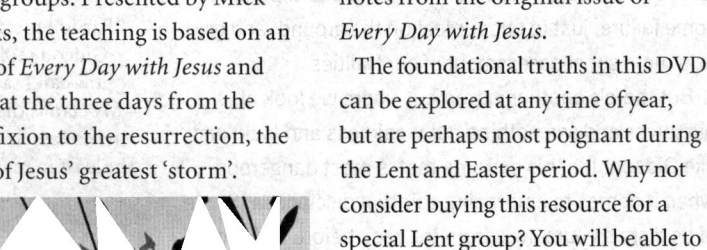

CWR also has other DVD resources particularly suitable for the Lent and Easter period. *Jesus - the Wounded Healer*, again presented by Mick Brooks, is filmed on location at Wintershall Estate in Surrey with footage from their famous *Life of Christ* open-air production.

Then there are two resources with Jeff Lucas in his *Life Journeys* series, *The Impossible Dream?* and *Singing in the Rain*. All three of these DVDs are available for £19.99 each incl VAT and also come with an accompanying booklet, additional copies of which can be bought separately for £3.50 each to facilitate group study.

'These DVDs add a whole new dimension to a Lent Group study. They bring the subject matter to life in a way that a written study cannot. The discussion starters in the accompanying book provide a really helpful structure for group discussion, and the Bible-reading notes are perfect for cementing and expanding the learning in your own time during the following week.'

Jesus – The Wounded Healer
Presented by Mick Brooks
EAN: 5027957001350

Life Journeys – The Impossible Dream?
Presented by Jeff Lucas
EAN: 5027957001268

Life Journeys – Singing in the Rain
Presented by Jeff Lucas
EAN: 5027957001183

19/20 JAN

Hebrews 2:17–18 // Philippians 2:1–11

Jesus and disciplines

It's an idea that recurs in Christian circles – that Jesus lived life on earth with the distinct advantage of being God. So He only asked questions to benefit the person being questioned – He already knew the answers. The idea is that, being fully God and fully man, He knew everything – He was omniscient. But surely that would mean He would also have to have been omnipresent as well – at all places at all times? Why the need for travel?

Although He did discern things about people supernaturally, He decided not to use the 'God card', but to live with the help of the Holy Spirit, in exactly the same way as we do. That's why His temptation was a triumph – He won as a human being just like us, through the power of the Holy Spirit, whose power is available fully to us too. In His humanity, He grew tired, He aged, He got thirsty, hungry, experienced joy, pressure and tension. Jesus won in life through walking with the Father, and using disciplines of prayer, fasting, service and Sabbath. His example is for real.

To ponder: What would you say to the person who says that Jesus was 'God with skin on'?

… He won as a human being …

MON 21 JAN

Gradual life change

BIG PICTURE
1 Corinthians 9:25
Galatians 5:22–26

FOCUS:
'Everyone who competes in the games goes into strict training.'
(1 Cor. 9:25)

IT'S the classic dilemma of the dieter – and I am one of them. We read the latest book about the new weight-loss revolution idea, and then throw ourselves into a new regime that means we will eat few carbs, little fat or lots of pineapple. We may even take on alarmingly large quantities of cabbage soup, and lose weight and friends simultaneously. The dilemma emerges when we reach our target; now, if we're not very careful, we start to slip back into old, unhealthy eating patterns. Once we marched resolutely past the crisp packets in the supermarket; suddenly we find ourselves consuming a multi-pack in one sitting. Diligence is required; lifestyle change, permanent healthy eating, and not just yo-yo dieting. No wonder Paul talks about training – one meaning of the word is 'striving'. There's nothing casual or accidental about the results that disciplined living brings.

Sometimes Christians emphasise epic encounters and massive junction moments, which are wonderful. But surely life change happens, not just because of moments of revolution, but as a result of taking thousands of daily decisions, prompted by truth and fuelled by grace. The English Standard Version renders Paul's words as 'every athlete exercises self-control in all things'. We touched on this earlier, but let's be reminded: spiritual discipline is rounded healthy living. It's not that we pray a lot, and gossip endlessly too; that we are diligent about diet, and lazy about generosity; God calls us to be intentional about all areas of our lives.

Prayer: Lord, help me to live as an awake, alert and intentional person today, choosing well. Amen.

TUES 22 JAN

Mental discipline

BIG PICTURE
2 Corinthians 10:1–5
1 Peter 1:13–16

FOCUS:
'We demolish arguments and every pretension that sets itself up against the knowledge of God, and we take captive every thought to make it obedient to Christ.'
(2 Cor. 10:5)

I HAVE a runaway mind. Never short of ideas (many of which are exhausting and impractical), my brain runs at high speed. I think I dream vividly because it takes a few hours for my brain to cool down. I'm glad to have a high-velocity mind: it has given me many innovative ideas. But my strength is also my weakness. Imagination can spark anxiety; some of my happier days have suddenly clouded over as my mind crashes into fear, speculation and even despair.

My runaway mind goes into warp speed when I am out running. Suddenly I can think of too many reasons to slow down, stop, curl up on the pavement and order a pizza. But just as I can choose not to order a calorie explosion for a meal, so I can choose to 'arrest' or take my thoughts captive. We are not to be at the mercy of every stray notion that sneaks into our consciousness, but can choose what we will mull over. Paul's words to the Philippians can help us here: 'whatever is true, whatever is noble, whatever is right, whatever is pure, whatever is lovely, whatever is admirable – if anything is excellent or praiseworthy – think about such things' (Phil. 4:8). And his reference to 'taking thoughts captive' is a military metaphor that carries the image of a sword, and leading a series of captive soldiers away to a secure citadel. We're called to lead our thoughts and make them bow to the Lordship of Christ. Perhaps you've allowed some runaway thoughts to wreak havoc in your mind lately. Draw that sword, and arrest them now, before they spoil another precious day.

Prayer: Help me to identify unhelpful patterns of thought that repeatedly infiltrate my mind, Lord. Amen.

WED 23 JAN

Hard work and Church pillars

BIG PICTURE
1 Corinthians 9:25
1 Corinthians 7:1–9

FOCUS:
'Everyone who competes in the games goes into strict training.'
(1 Cor. 9:25)

IT'S a description that has frequently been used to honour those who faithfully serve among God's people: 'They're a real pillar of the Church.' This does not mean they are like stone pillars – cold, unmovable and in the way, although we have all met – or been – Christians who sadly fit that description.

Church 'pillars' are to be found everywhere. Hardworking, sacrificing themselves without fuss, they frequently shoulder burdens and responsibilities beyond what they're called to. Sometimes they go over the top. It is not right for us to spend all our lives exhausting ourselves, bustling around from one church activity to the next. But I wonder if the pendulum has swung too far in the other direction; now we're nervous of any cause that might be too demanding.

Tertullian, commending the example of the athletes to persecuted Christians, says, 'They are constrained, harassed, wearied.'[1] The athlete deliberately puts his body through rigorous, punishing routines in order to excel. Perhaps you're serving to the point of exhaustion, and you'd like to throw in the towel and just put your feet up. After all, there are plenty who do. While it might be good to slow down, it's good to be tired – to spend ourselves – for the sake of the kingdom of God.

By the way, the other place where Paul uses the word 'temperate' is where he talks about sexual self-control in 1 Corinthians 7. 'If it feels good, do it' is obviously not a biblical mandate: on the contrary. Instead, we're called to *do* good, whatever we feel.

Prayer: Lord, help me to choose what is right, rather than what I feel I want to do. Amen.

1. M.R. Vincent, *Word Studies in the New Testament (1 Cor. 9:25)* (Bellingham, WA: Logos Research Systems Inc, 2002).

… it's good to be tired … for the sake of the kingdom of God

THURS 24 JAN

Playing by the rules

BIG PICTURE
2 Timothy 2:5
2 Thessalonians 3:10

FOCUS:
'Similarly, anyone who competes as an athlete does not receive the victor's crown except by competing according to the rules.' (2 Tim. 2:5)

RULES is another unfashionable word, like temperance. Some Christians wrongly insist that, because of grace, there are no longer any rules to live by, which is a complete misunderstanding, as Paul clearly pointed out in Romans. When he writes of being 'disqualified' (1 Cor. 9:27), he uses the word 'castaway', the term used in the games to refer to an athlete disqualified by the judges because of cheating. Athletes competing in the ancient games had to swear by their gods that they would train hard and play by the rules. In choosing to be followers of Christ, we too have pledged our allegiance – to God.

Just as an athlete will be disqualified if they launch into the race before the starting pistol has been fired, or stray into another runner's lane, so we must know, as the people of God, we are called to play by the rules of purity, kindness, trustworthiness, loyalty and a host of other virtues.

Perhaps some of us find ourselves in turmoil right now, because we know very well what we need to do – it's just that we don't want to. When that crisis comes, obedience is required. Jesus comes to us as Lord, not as a spiritual advisor. When the football coach stands on the sidelines, and shouts commands and strategies, he is not offering advice. He expects immediate action. And just before using the metaphor of athlete, Paul uses a military metaphor to urge Timothy to faithfulness: soldiers are those under strict command. As one writer wryly commented, 'Moses didn't come down from the mountain with the Ten Suggestions.'

Jesus comes to us as Lord …

Prayer: Lord, when I know what to do, but really don't want to embrace obedience, help me to play by the rules. Amen.

FRI 25 JAN

Running aimlessly

BIG PICTURE
1 Corinthians 9:25–26
2 Corinthians 5:1–10

FOCUS:
'Therefore I do not run like someone running aimlessly.' (1 Cor. 9:26)

WE'RE jumping forward just a little, because some commentators believe that Paul's phrase, 'I do not run aimlessly', was linked with yesterday's metaphor about playing by the rules. The picture of an athlete zig-zagging down the track, obstructing the lanes of fellow competitors, is deliberately absurd. It is a call to continual focus, and adjustment. But here I am really challenged, because it is possible to go through all the 'right' routines of the Christian life, church attendance, Bible study, active service within the church and outside, yet be in 'cruise control' mode, drifting rather than actively pursuing God's purposes. It's a deceptive place to be – a runner drifting into other lanes would soon be noticed and disqualified – but we can settle into a sedentary Christianity, which neither actively denies our belief nor affirms it. Surely it's good to take stock regularly and reflect on our progress, lest we just amble along, getting nowhere.

And if we're to avoid running aimlessly, let's consider what it is that we're aiming for, apart from the rewards and prizes that we'll consider in more detail later. Broadly, we make it our aim to please God daily (2 Cor. 5:9). This means that we will be careful not to get distracted by unhelpful entanglements (2 Tim. 2:4). We will attempt to do things ethically, both in the sight of God and others (2 Cor. 8:21). And as we live purposefully, our prayer is that others will want to emulate our example (2 Tim. 3:10). Aiming right will keep us on track.

Prayer: May I be fully awake and alert, focused on my aim today, Lord. Amen.

26/27 JAN

1 Corinthians 9:25–26 // Acts 18:18

A personal rule

We've already seen that we are called to run by the rules of the race if we're to be winners. Rules don't equal legalism. On the contrary, many have found it helpful to develop a personal 'rule of life'. This is a thoughtful, prayerful series of personal decisions that we might embrace: helpful choices to enable us to run well. We do not inflict them on others – that leads to legalism. What would a personalised rule of life mean for you? It might mean that you choose always to be reading a book – perhaps two at a time, one Christian, one not. You might decide, if you drink alcohol, that you will only do so at weekends; that you'll walk each morning; be disciplined about not speaking critically of others. You might develop a personal plan to give, to the church and to those in need, or take a disciplined approach to offering hospitality, being intentional each month in inviting a new person from the church – or a neighbour from down the road – for a meal. Paul had obviously taken a vow which involved a haircut: more details are not known, but this was obviously part of a personal rule in his life.

What might a rule of life look like for you?

To ponder: Take ten minutes to begin building the basics of a realistic and achievable experimental 'rule of life' for the next month of your life.

Rules don't equal legalism

MON 28 JAN

A fading crown

BIG PICTURE
1 Corinthians 9:25–26
James 4:14

FOCUS:
'They do it to get a crown that will not last.'
(1 Cor. 9:25)

SITTING with some friends discussing our elderly parents, one of the group commented that his 91-year-old mother was absolutely loving her life. 'I expect she's looking forward to heaven', someone else said, knowing that the lady is a Christian. 'No, she's just lapping up every moment of her life right here', came the honest reply.

I was encouraged, because I find it incredibly difficult to live 'in the light of eternity', to use a phrase much loved by preachers. Perhaps if would be different if I was living under the threat of persecution, or battling a painful disease. When Paul spoke those famous words about living for Christ, and knowing that dying was gain (Phil. 1:21), he spoke as an exhausted veteran who was looking forward to being with Christ at last – a welcome release from all the battles he had endured. But as I write this, on a gloriously (albeit rare) summery day in England, I am keen to live for as long as possible, to see my grandchildren grow up and have children of their own; to accomplish as yet unreached goals that I feel God has placed in my heart; to enjoy and embrace the twilight years, and then the sunset of my life. So it's a timely reminder to remember that, as good as life can be, it's not always going to be like this, and that we have decided to live for something that will last for ever.

The athletes worked hard for a crown that would soon wither. Perhaps that's what living in the light of eternity means; that we prioritise, invest in, and work for that which will last for always.

Prayer: Father, please show me what it really means to live in the light of eternity. Amen.

TUES 29 JAN

An eternal crown

BIG PICTURE
1 Corinthians 9:25–26
James 1:2–12

FOCUS:
'… but we do it to get a crown that will last for ever.' (1 Cor. 9:25)

JUNE 23rd, 1978. It was a much anticipated event, as graduation day dawned at the Bible college I attended. But we were not to know that it would be quite unforgettable for terrible, tragic reasons. The preacher for the graduation ceremony was Peter Griffiths, who had travelled from Zimbabwe (then Rhodesia). As he drove through the leafy lanes of Surrey to our school, he did not know that all his colleagues back in Africa had been brutally murdered by some terrorists who had entered the mission compound. Told the terrible news on arrival, Peter went on to preach one of the most memorable sermons I have ever heard, based on Paul's words that I mentioned yesterday, 'For me to live is Christ, to die is gain.'

One of the missionaries, knowing that the end was near, tried to comfort her fellow martyrs as they endured their last minutes on this earth. She cried out 'Don't worry, they can't kill the soul!' Paul, always aware that more beatings, imprisonment or martyrdom might not be far off, lived with a similar affirmation.

I'm very conscious that some readers of *Life Every Day* are living in the wintry season of uncertainty, which at times tempts you to despair. Perhaps you are waiting for test results, and if the answer is what you fear, then the outlook, for this life, is not great. Without clichés or slogans, I pray that you will have a peace that comes from knowing that Christ has gone on ahead of you, and beaten death for ever. And therefore a crown – for ever – awaits.

Prayer: Lord, I pray for those in the valley of trial. Give them strength for today, and bright hope for tomorrow. Amen.

'For me to live is Christ, to die is gain'

WED 30 JAN

Witnesses

BIG PICTURE
Hebrews 11:1–12:3
Hebrews 6:12

FOCUS:
'Therefore, since we are surrounded by such a great cloud of witnesses ... let us run with perseverance the race marked out for us.' (Heb. 12:1)

THERE'S a lot of scholarly debate about what exactly the writer to the Hebrews means by saying we are 'surrounded by such a great cloud of witnesses'. Having identified some Old Testament heroes of the faith (with quite a few surprising names, such as Rahab the harlot and Samson), the writer spurs the Hebrews on to run well; the picture evokes images of a crowd cheering from the stands and seats of a stadium. But that might be a misconception; although some think that this means that they are actually watching our progress. Perhaps they groan when we fail or misunderstand, or cheer when we get something right. Others think that idea stretches the analogy too far, and that it is their testimony to the faithfulness of God, rather than their observation, that should inspire us now that it's our turn on the track. The thought is that they proved God faithful in their circumstances; their sacrifices were proven to be worthwhile, and so whatever faith costs us, their stories encourage us to do what's right.

However we interpret these words, we must not miss their encouragement. We are not pioneers of the faith, but stand in a noble line of those who have exercised faith and been found faithful. Whether they observe our daily lives or not (which I doubt) the truth is this: we run as runners in an epic relay. Others have handed the baton to us, and, with God at their side, have navigated safely through storms of unbelief, fear, shame and a host of other challenges. God brought them through, and He is our God too.

Prayer: Others have proved You faithful, Lord, and have been found faithful. May the same be true of me. Amen.

WAVERLEY IN THE SPRING

Spring is a wonderful season for planning time away to be equipped with insights and skills to help you grow in God, and Waverley Abbey House in Farnham, Surrey is the perfect venue. A beautiful Georgian house set in a delightful country setting, it's a great place to relax, spend time with God and meet others. CWR has a Spring Programme packed full of residential courses which could inspire and encourage you throughout 2013 and beyond.

In February we have another popular Bible Discovery Course led by Philip Greenslade called **Let's go up to Easter**. During this weekend you will have the opportunity to reflect on the Songs of Ascent – Psalms 120–134, exploring some of these moving and intense psalms. Join us for this weekend of scriptural and spiritual reflection.

As we move into March we will be holding a **Preparation for Marriage weekend**, and later in the month running our five-day programme, **Pastoral Care in the Local Church**. This course gives delegates an insight into how to help others achieve their true potential in Christ within His Church. You will be envisioned with a biblical understanding of pastoral care and helped to develop your skills for caring for others, as well as being shown how to handle challenging people ... and much more.

The following week is our **Introduction to Biblical Care and Counselling**, another five-day course during which you will learn how God has designed us to live, why problems develop and how to begin to help others. This can be a life-transforming few days as you learn how to apply the biblical principles taught to your own life.

We have people booking on courses from all over Europe and further afield, and we do hope that wherever you are you will decide to book a visit to Waverley in the spring!

Waverley Spring Programme
- Let's go up to Easter – 15–17 February 2013
- Preparation for Marriage – 1–3 March 2013
- Pastoral Care in the Local Church – 11–15 March 2013
- Introduction to Biblical Care and Counselling – 18–22 March 2013

For further information or to book visit www.cwr.org.uk/training or call +44 (0)1252 784719.

THURS 31 JAN

Throw off what hinders

BIG PICTURE
Hebrews 12:1
1 Corinthians 6:12

FOCUS:
'... let us throw off everything that hinders ...' (Heb. 12:1)

NO SENSIBLE runner would think of competing with excess weight – that would obviously hamper progress. In ancient times, many runners would compete naked, rather than be hampered by clothing. In recent years, there's been considerable debate in the swimming world, because new technology has produced swimsuit designs that are literally race changers: weight and aerodynamics make the difference between winners and losers.

The text here literally means *to lay aside superfluous flesh*. It refers to the strict diet that runners embraced to be as lean and lithe as healthily possible. The idea of throwing aside what hinders points us to a vital truth: some things are not necessarily sinful, just unhelpful. As one writer says, 'There are some things which are not expressly forbidden, but whose results are such as to rule them out for the believer.'[1]

I often pause for breath before rushing to speak, and ask, 'Is what I'm about to say helpful?' Or this verse might challenge us in the use of our time. Hobbies are important. But I've known people who have become so fanatically obsessed with their hobbies that their commitment to them has damaged their family and church life. Then there are those who, considering a year of mission, might decide that while they are perfectly entitled to pursue a relationship, it would be a distraction and therefore a hindrance during that time. Let's not just think in terms of right and wrong, but also consider what's helpful or a distraction.

Prayer: Gracious God, give me a heart that knows both what is wrong and what will hinder. Help me throw aside any weight. Amen.

1. D. Prior, *The Message of 1 Corinthians: Life in the local church*, The Bible Speaks Today series (Leicester: IVP, 1996).

FRI 01 FEB

The sin that so easily entangles

BIG PICTURE
Hebrews 12:1
James 1:19–25

FOCUS:
'... and the sin that so easily entangles.'
(Heb. 12:1)

IT WOULD be a total disaster. If the athlete decided to run clothed, rather than naked, as we discussed yesterday, then his robe could eventually slide down and catch around the ankles, tripping him up. Tangled up in his own wayward clothing, the runner concedes defeat. This is the portrait painted by the term, 'the sin that so easily entangles'. Martin Luther called it 'the sin which so easily clings to us'. We might think of it as a besetting sin.

There are some temptations that never stop by to visit me. It's just simply not in my make-up or character to want what's being offered. But I know full well that there are areas of weakness in my life that could lead me to disaster. Over the years, my tussle with those temptations has become a familiar fight. Those are the areas that I need to especially guard when I'm tired or discouraged. In the case of the Hebrews, their 'besetting sin' was a reluctance to put their faith in Jesus as Messiah and Saviour. It is helpful to know that, because we often think of besetting sins as being habits or patterns of behaviour that are overtly morally wrong. In fact, the context of this encouragement is to avoid a pattern of unbelief.

We're called to diligence as we run. One translator says the meaning here is of 'the sins that stand around us', and paints a picture of hungry animals circling a campfire, waiting for a moment to strike. Do we know what our besetting sins are? Does anyone else know? How tragic it is to see a winner trip and fall headlong. But the trip can be avoided.

Prayer: Lord, help me to know myself, as Your Spirit shows me. Father, what sin could so easily entangle itself around me? Amen.

Do we know what our besetting sins are?

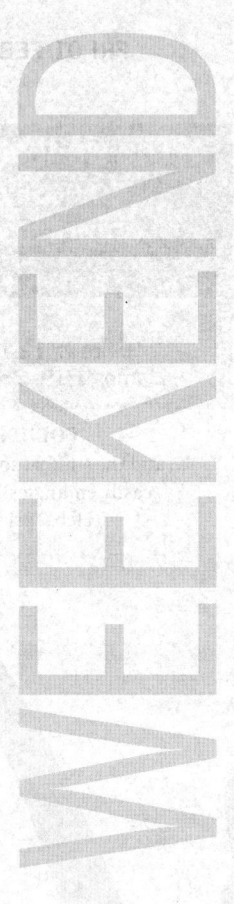

02/03 FEB

Hebrews 12:1 // John 6:60–71

Run with perseverance

It was one of the rare hot summer Sundays. I was glad to be in church, but together with other perspiring worshippers, was finding it difficult to focus. Something about the vocabulary of the service worried me: every new announcement was about an 'amazing' happening, an 'epic' event, and the leader kept asking us if we were excited. Many dutifully replied that they were, although it did seem more like they were reading a script than making a heartfelt confession.

Christianity is not always exciting. There are times when God speaks, moves, or answers a prayer in spectacular fashion. But the idea that this is a daily experience is false. Scripture has a lot to say about faith, which is exciting, but a lot too about endurance. There are times when we don't feel we have much to say to God: life's dullness or difficulties render us speechless. I'm encouraged by the resolute response of some of the disciples of Jesus, who determined to follow Him, because, when it came to words of eternity, they knew there was nowhere else to go. Perseverance is part of every race.

To ponder: Do we make the daily Christian life sound more exciting than it really is?

Christianity is not always exciting

MON 04 FEB

Run the race marked out for us

BIG PICTURE
Hebrews 12:1
John 21:15–23

FOCUS:
'And let us run with perseverance the race marked out for us ...'
(Heb. 12:1)

IT'S a temptation that I can easily succumb to – fretting about the inconsistencies of other Christians. It can happen when I am a guest preacher at a church, and the theology from the platform is foolish or deficient, or maybe the language would be completely incomprehensible to an outsider. It's right that I notice these things: I am called to help the churches that I serve to be more effective, and I don't serve them well if I ignore obvious frailties. But there comes a point when I am not so much alerted to the failings of the church, but irritated or even demoralised by them. And dwelling on them drives me to discouragement.

As we hear the writer to the Hebrews exhort us to 'run the race marked out for us', the phrasing suggests that we each have a unique path, a specific way to serve the kingdom of God. Whether that's the exact meaning of the sentence (and frankly we are not sure of the precise meaning), it's certainly true that it takes me plenty of focus to stay 'on track' myself, without becoming unhealthily preoccupied with the wanderings and wobbling of others.

Perhaps like Peter in his relationship with Jesus and John the beloved, you're currently asking 'What about him?' – you are more concerned than you should be about someone else's walk with the Lord. Jesus' response to you is blunt: 'What is that to you? You must follow me.' May God show us which lane we are supposed to be running in – and then keep us within the white lines. Constant preoccupation with the way that others are running will not help us to stay straight.

Prayer: Lord, help me know the difference between concern for others, and unhealthy preoccupation with the way they run the race. Amen.

TUES 05 FEB

The pacesetter

BIG PICTURE
Hebrews 12:1–2
John 1:1–18

FOCUS:
'... fixing our eyes on Jesus, the pioneer and perfecter of faith.' (Heb. 12:2)

IT'S probably the most famous run of all time, when the barrier of the four-minute mile was finally smashed by Roger Bannister in 1954. What might not be so well known is that Bannister was helped by two pacesetters, who ran ahead of him, and then dropped out of the race, knowing that he alone could maintain such a punishing rate. Pacesetters not only allow the athlete who follows them to relax, knowing that they are running at the appropriate speed, but they also take the brunt of wind resistance.

Jesus has gone ahead of us, living a life of obedience to the Father in exactly the same way as we do; we saw earlier that our tendency to think that He played an extra trump card as Messiah and Son of God is misleading, robbing us of the true impact of His wonderful example. He is the author of life itself (Acts 3:15), who completely won the prize of our salvation. All that He did, He did by faith, as He completely obeyed the will of the Father. We don't run in front, but with Him as the leader of the pack.

And it's only as I follow in His wake that the winning run is possible. Sometimes my Christianity becomes hard work, because I insist on spending my energy pursuing my good ideas, often sprinting forward in presumption, rather than committing my ways to Him. The Church throughout the ages has tried to make the mission of God her mission, with disastrous results. His job is to lead; our task is to follow, today.

Let's make sure that the pacesetter is truly out in front, and stays in that pole position.

His job is to lead; our task is to follow ...

Prayer: When presumption edges me ahead of You, or disobedience causes me to lag way behind, help me to get back in step with You, Lord. Amen.

WED 06 FEB

Eyes on Jesus

BIG PICTURE
Hebrews 12:1–2
Psalm 25:1–15

FOCUS:
'… fixing our eyes on Jesus, the pioneer and perfecter of faith.'
(Heb. 12:2)

THERE was a much loved song when I first became a Christian: 'Open my eyes Lord, I want to see Jesus.' It filled me with a disconcerting cocktail of hope and despair, because no matter how much I crunched my eyes shut and tried to focus, I couldn't see Jesus. How do you see one who is alive but invisible? But here we are not being exhorted to seek a mystical spiritual experience, but rather to consider our pacesetter, Christ. The word means 'to focus our minds upon', and we're shown some of the key aspects of the work of Christ that we should remember, especially when the race is hard. These include His endurance (as He ran the marathon of the Crucifixion), and His triumph – He sat down at the right hand of God. He pushed through the 'wall' of pain, even as the crowd jeered, rather than cheered, and then went up to receive a throne. There He is seated, because the work has been done, once and for all. Never again will He have to stand to work for our salvation: everything that needs to be done has been completed.

The word 'looking' also has a sense of distance about it, which I think is helpful, although it is not saying that God is a long way away. Sometimes we find ourselves focusing on what hems us in, and is very close at hand. Faith enables us to look over and beyond this, to what seems far away, yet is so real.

As Corrie Ten Boom, who served Christ faithfully in the midst of the holocaust, put it, 'Faith is like radar that sees through the fog, the reality of things at a distance that the human eye cannot see.'[1]

Prayer: Lord, may I be able to look up and beyond whatever is hemming me in, to the glory of You. Amen.

1. Corrie Ten Boom, *The Hiding Place* (London: Bantam Books, 1984).

THURS 07 FEB

Consider Him

BIG PICTURE
Hebrews 12:3
Galatians 6:1–10

FOCUS:
'Consider him who endured such opposition from sinners, so that you will not grow weary and lose heart.' (Heb. 12:3)

WE ALL need heroes. Their stories of courage can move us emotionally, and inspire us to believe that we can do excellent things as well. The writer to the Hebrews encourages us to 'consider' Jesus and His faithfulness in the face of such terrible suffering. As we pause to do that, let's remind ourselves once again that Jesus faced trouble and pain in exactly the same way as we do. At the risk of repetition, it's so important that we realise that Jesus faced His awful execution as a man; all that we might feel if we were close to death went through His heart and mind. We know that He sought support from His closest friends, and prayer was a mainstay as He wrestled in Gethsemane.

As we ponder His faithfulness, we should be encouraged, rather than grow weary. The picture painted by these words is that of an athlete who crosses the finish line and then, utterly spent, throws himself on the ground, unable to take a single step more. The word 'consider' comes from the same word as the one that gives us the word 'logarithm' and has to do with calculations. The writer is saying, when you suffer, make sure that the suffering, faithful Jesus is at the centre of your mental calculations. Easier said than done, but surely possible with the help of God's Spirit.

Perhaps you feel that you're trekking uphill right now, and you've hit the dreaded wall. My prayer is that, as you consider that Jesus went all the way, and completed the mission, you will find grace and strength to cross the finish line too.

Prayer: Lord, grant me eyes to see what I cannot see, and what seems far off. Amen.

SAUL, destined to become Paul, did not have a gentle, gradual conversion. Grabbed by God, metaphorically thrown off his high horse on the Damascus Road, he was blinded by Jesus' brilliance. God seized him not only to stop the terrible persecution he was instigating, but for positive kingdom purposes. Right at the start, it was made clear: the former firebrand would become the apostle to the Gentiles. That was his new calling. He was also called to know Christ, just like the twelve apostles, who were called to be *with* Jesus as well as be *sent out* by Jesus (Mark 3:14). Paul was called to function as an apostle, and to relationship as a friend and brother of Christ.

BIG PICTURE
Philippians 3:1–14
Acts 9:1–15

FOCUS:
'... I press on to take hold of that for which Christ Jesus took hold of me.'
(Phil. 3:12)

Although we all know that we are called to that primary purpose of knowing Christ by faith, finding the broader purposes and the will of God for our lives is not always easy. We need to keep asking as our lives unfold: what have you called me for and to, Lord? For what purpose am I on the earth right now? Again, there's a general answer to that question that is the same for all of us, whatever our work or vocation: we are called to serve the purposes of the kingdom of God. But surely we are also created for specific aspects of the kingdom mission. Let's keep asking that we might be people of purpose, and that we might fulfil the purposes of God, whether we are fully aware that we are doing so or not. Sometimes we are right in the centre of what God wants us to do, but He doesn't send an email of confirmation.

Prayer: I specifically make myself available to You and to Your purposes, Lord. May I take hold of that for which You have taken hold of me. Amen.

... what have you called me for and to, Lord?

09/10 FEB

Philippians 3:1–14 // Ephesians 4:1–16

One thing

Earlier, when we were talking about the role of the pacesetter, I mentioned Roger Bannister, who first broke the four-minute-mile record. But there was another famous race day in 1954, when Bannister was set to run against the only other man who had broken the four-minute barrier, John Landy.

Landy had gained a substantial lead, and did not know where Bannister was on the track as they headed for the finish line. The crowd roared, and Landy, unable to hear Bannister's footfall, took a moment to look back – and that cost him the race. Bannister surged past and won by a five-yard margin. It is obvious that if we're going to be winners in the race, we need to face the front, but it's such a common tactical error by so many Christians, it's worth pondering for a few days. As we'll see, we can spend our days looking over our shoulders, in regret, in shame – which not only robs us of the joy of today, and being fully present in the moment, but also breaks our focus upon Christ. We become obsessed with where we have been, not where He is. Paul was determined – so should we be.

… we need to face the front …

To ponder: Sometimes Christians use the phrase, 'Let go and let God'. How does that square with Paul's focused decisiveness here?

CWR CONFERENCING

CWR's two conference venues, Waverley Abbey House in Farnham, Surrey and Pilgrim Hall in Uckfield, East Sussex, make ideal venues for your church weekends, Alpha Away Days, Leadership meetings and training events. Both are set in spacious grounds in the midst of beautiful countryside.

Waverley Abbey House
- Day meetings for up to 100 people
- Residential accommodation for up to 44 people
- Eight meeting/conference rooms
- Dining room
- Lounge and coffee bar with pool table
- Patios with outdoor seating
- Views across tranquil lake to woodlands and ruins of ancient Waverley Abbey

Waverely Abbey House, Waverley Lane, Farnham, Surrey GU9 8EP

Call our Bookings Team on
01252 784733
or email waverley@cwr.org.uk

Pilgrim Hall
- Day meetings for up to 125 people
- Residential accommodation for up to 110 people
- Three lounges and two dining rooms
- Conservatory overlooking the grounds
- Table tennis, pool table and table football
- Heated outdoor swimming pool (May–October)
- Tennis court, putting green and croquet lawn
- Outdoor seating and summer house

Pilgrim Hall, Easons Green, Uckfield, East Sussex TN22 5RE

Call our Bookings Team on 01825 840295
or email pilgrim@cwr.org.uk

www.cwr.org.uk/conferencing

MON 11 FEB

Looking back – at shame

BIG PICTURE
Philippians 3:13–14
Acts 22:1–21

FOCUS:
'… forgetting what is behind …' (Phil. 3:13)

IF EVER someone could have been completely immobilised in the race, it was Paul. His murderous past meant that he could have disqualified himself before he got started. His twisted religious zeal was the catalyst for the deaths of many Christians, and the scattering of the church in Jerusalem. I wonder if, in his darker seasons, he ever dreamed about dying Stephen, the Church's first martyr, pounded to a terrible death by a lynch mob – urged on by Paul. And when he went to Antioch to co-lead the church there with Barnabas, Paul would have come face to face with many of the people who were only in Antioch as a result of that first persecution. Incredibly, the man who had hounded them like a wolf had now become their shepherd. Quite apart from the tension that this could have created, Paul would have been reminded daily of his terrible days as Saul.

Somehow, Paul managed to free himself from the taunting memories of his history. Although he never forgot where he came from, in terms of his history and testimony, it seems that for the most part he was able to rise above the shame of what he had been and done.

Sometimes grace and forgiveness become a theory, an almost too-good-to-be-true theological idea that we believe in, in an abstract way, but don't apply to our own journeys, especially when it comes to actions that we are deeply embarrassed or ashamed about. But we'll never be able to run well unless we determine to obey God, by accepting His once and for all verdict about our sins: they are forgiven.

Prayer: Forgiving God, teach me how to submit to Your verdict of forgiveness for the things that especially shame me. Amen.

TUES 12 FEB

Straining forward

BIG PICTURE
Philippians 3:13–14
Hebrews 6:1

FOCUS:
'... and straining towards what is ahead ...'
(Phil. 3:13)

THE picture of straining towards what is ahead is one of a chariot rider who leans forward, every sinew and muscle urging the horses to greater speed. Or, to change the sporting event, it's the aerodynamically perfect posture of the sprinter, body angled forward to the maximum efficiency to enable him to breast the winning tape first. It's a portrait of tension, of utter engagement and focus. There's nothing relaxed about this posture. That kind of intentionality is mandatory in the Christian race as a whole (faith on cruise control doesn't work, which is why the New Testament constantly calls us to be alert and attentive) and because it takes determination to focus forwards. Yesterday we talked about shame; instinctively it's easy for us to live chained to our greatest mistakes.

We're taught to be suspicious of free gifts, and our feelings of shame can swamp us. It takes gritty determination not to wallow in our failure, mental discipline that enables us to say an emphatic 'No' when we're tempted to look back to our past. A sense of peace about all our yesterdays doesn't just land upon us, but needs to be taken, received by faith.

Accepting forgiveness is not a passive act: it takes active faith as we determine to submit to God's verdict of gracious pardon. What is it in your history that tends to demand your renewed focus and attention, usually just when you are trying to get focus on what is or what's ahead? It's time to lean forward, not look back.

Prayer: Lord, help me not just to ask for forgiveness, but to take it with a firm grip, so that I might lean forward into what's ahead. Amen.

It's time to lean forward, not look back

WED 13 FEB

Looking back – living in the past

BIG PICTURE
Philippians 3:4–7
Philippians 3:13–14

FOCUS:
'… forgetting what is behind …' (Phil. 3:13)

AS WE saw yesterday, Paul had some skeletons in his cupboard that he needed to leave behind – literally. As a persecutor of the Church he was responsible for scattering the Church and shedding a lot of innocent blood. But we're wrong to think that his past was just negative. His testimony to the Philippians was that he had been a Pharisee, which would have placed him in a position of respect and prominence. Not only that, but the reason that he was able to push forward persecution was because he had a prominent role in the religious hierarchy, with authority and power. All of this was lost when he had begun his marathon race with Jesus. Past friendships and alliances would have been shattered. Those who had once looked up to him now looked down on him with disdain, pity and even hatred, seeing him as a traitor to the Pharisaic cause. But he was determined not to live with regret about what he had lost, but rather to reckon, or calculate, it as trash.

I once prayed with a man who was tormented by the memory of an illicit relationship that he had prior to his marriage. Images of the intimacy that he had enjoyed kept clouding his mind, distracting him from his marriage as he fantasised and focused on what used to be. But with careful discipline, and as he made himself accountable to his friends, he gradually found freedom from the more 'attractive' elements of his history. Letting bygones be bygones is easier said than done, but it can be accomplished.

Prayer: Lord, help me to leave that which I once found enjoyable, whether it was good or bad, behind. Amen.

Letting bygones be bygones is easier said than done …

THURS 14 FEB

Nostalgia

BIG PICTURE
Philippians 3:13–14
Zechariah 2:1–5

FOCUS:
'… forgetting what is behind …' (Phil. 3:13)

IT WAS one of those conversations that came out of nowhere, but I'll never forget it. We were sharing dinner with a couple from our church, and they were remembering, with great affection, the 'good old days' when everybody knew each other, when the church was a very close, tight-knit family, and where if you were going through a difficult patch, it wasn't just that people would pray for you on request. So close was the congregation that they usually already knew what you were going through, and volunteered their help and prayer. And this couple knew first hand what it meant to go through the darkest seasons, in the sudden illness and death of their beautiful daughter. But, as he wiped away a stray tear, the still-grieving dad said that they had been willing to surrender that closeness, because of the thousands that were being reached by the church now. It wasn't just that he refused to get stuck in superficial nostalgia about the loss of pews or the times of the service altering: he had let go of something that was very precious because he was committed to the mission.

When the past has been good, we can revere it inappropriately (and often think of it as being better than it really was). We become like the man in Zechariah 2:1–5 who wanted to conduct a survey of the ruins of Jerusalem, allowing yesterday's glories and past failures to determine the dimensions of the future. Let's be grateful for history, and even celebrate it, but never allow it to become a shackle that prevents us embracing our future or what God has for us today.

Prayer: Help me to celebrate and be grateful for great aspects of the past, but never make an idol of what was, Lord. Amen.

FRI 15 FEB

No turning back

BIG PICTURE
Luke 9:57–62
Matthew 4:18–22

FOCUS:
'Jesus replied, "No one who puts a hand to the plough and looks back is fit for service in the kingdom of God."'
(Luke 9:62)

IT'S a jaunty song: 'I have decided to follow Jesus … no turning back, no turning back.' One writer isn't too keen on it, and wrote, 'I like the words. But sometimes I think the airy tune is inappropriate. It might be all right for Dorothy and the Tin Man as they skip along the Yellow Brick Road to Oz! But for followers of Christ, something martial might better fit the words.'[1]

Whatever our opinion of the song, it's important that we face the truth here: Jesus is letting us know that we're running in a marathon, not taking a stroll in the park. But as we read his words, we might be tempted to think that He is despising normal family relationships, having a home or any security. He is not, but rather is establishing a priority: these good and necessary things might, at times, need to be put on the line if we follow Christ. I remember a time when I was involved in a church that was passionate about church planting. Many people sold their homes, in a time of negative equity, and relocated just so that they could be part of the vision to take the gospel to another area. Their earthly security was not their priority, but the purposes of the kingdom of God had become their focus.

I'm challenged: when did I last experience discomfort or great cost for the cause of the kingdom? We can grumble when we're faced with the slightest inconvenience. And if we have paid a price, let's not lean on that as if that one season of sacrifice was all it takes. Perhaps it's time to carefully consider singing that song again in our current season of life.

Prayer: Lord, help me to keep putting my hand to the plough, in each unfolding time of my life. Amen.

1. R.K. Hughes, *Luke: That you may know the truth* (Wheaton, Illinois: Crossway Books, 1998) p.372.

16/17 FEB

Galatians 5:1–12 // Galatians 2:1–5

Beware of cheats

It happened at the Athens Olympics back in 2004. Vanderlei De Lima, from Brazil, was at the head of the marathon, just three miles from the finish, when he was attacked by a spectator, Cornelius Horan. The attack cost De Lima the race, and he finished third. Someone had cut in and that was that.

Paul writes about his friends in Galatia running well, but then is incensed that someone has 'cut in' on them, robbing them of their progress: 'You were running a good race. Who cut in on you to keep you from obeying the truth?' (Gal. 5:7).

It's a vivid picture, but with a surprise when you take a closer look. Those who hijacked the progress of the Galatian believers were not persecutors from outside of the church, but rather hyper-zealous Judaisers, who insisted that the rules and traditions of the old covenant be maintained. And so the Galatians, who had begun in the Spirit and in grace, have had their progress impeded. They have been 'cut up' and are going backwards, to works and the law. It isn't just sin that can seriously slow us down – so can intense, misguided, works-centred religion.

To ponder: Has your faith ever been 'cut up' by over-zealous legalism? What happened, and did you manage to escape its clutches?

DEAR LIFE EVERY DAY READER

FIRST OF ALL — THANK YOU!

Thanks for being part of the community that travels with me each day, as we share in these life application Bible notes together. As I trek around the UK and beyond, I often bump into *Life Every Day* readers, and so many of you share encouragement about how you find the notes helpful, sometimes timely, and practical. It feels as if we have a very real community together, focused on our reflections on Scripture. I'm grateful to you for being part of it.

Recently Kay and I have been feeling challenged about the need to call upon those who value our ministry for a greater level of prayerful support. I've not been terribly good at asking people to pray for us, and have realised that I've been remiss in this vital area. When I ponder the writings of Paul, I become aware that he saw the absolute necessity of asking his friends to stand with him in prayer. Repeatedly he asks them to pray for open doors, for boldness and for blessing as he preaches the good news of Jesus.

As Kay and I continue in our busy (sometimes frantic) ministry of preaching, writing and broadcasting we need your prayers and partnership. So I'd like to ask you to visit our website — now newly refurbished — (www.jefflucas.org) and click on the

LUCAS ON LIFE ...

box that says 'Partners'. That will take you to the area of the site that will explain how you might consider walking a little more closely with us in all that we're doing. We're hoping to be able to utilise the website, together with Twitter and Facebook, to send out occasional requests for prayer. We don't want to bombard you, but we'd like to include you if we may.

And as our ministry continues to expand it may be that you are one of those who can help us to respond to the opportunities that are emerging.

God bless you and yours today

Jeff

Recently Jeff recorded *Precepts of Leadership*, a 30-minute programme that will be shown in Russia, China, the Middle East, Australasia, Indonesia and Malaysia. Please pray that viewers, especially leaders, will be encouraged as they tune in.

Jeff also continues his broadcasting with Premier Radio and Revelation TV – see www.jefflucas.org for details.

MON 18 FEB

Hyper spirituality and the worship of angels

BIG PICTURE
Colossians 2:16–23
Matthew 23:1–4

FOCUS:
'Do not let anyone who delights in false humility and the worship of angels disqualify you.' (Col. 2:18)

I'VE seen it too many times. A church experiences a season of genuine Holy Spirit activity; their mission is effective, and their worship is energetic and exciting. Thank God. But in their place of blessing, they are also in a danger zone. Success brings its own temptations. Suddenly they no longer prioritise cooperation and unity with the other churches in their locality, because, as far as they're concerned, nobody else is as effective or as important to God as they are. Feeling that they are too busy, and have nothing to learn from others (and that they might be dragged down by what they perceive as being the others' stale mediocrity) they become isolated and arrogant. Now they are well along the path of self-deception, and might just need a visitation from Jesus to get an accurate diagnosis of their real condition, as the Laodiceans experienced (Rev. 3:14–22).

As Paul confronts those who are into false humility (probably some kind of mortification), he speaks of 'worship of the angels'. This is puzzling, because we know from wider Church history that the Church did not have a confused doctrine of angels at this period. So what did Paul refer to? It's possible that the 'worship of angels' refers to a claim by some that their worship was of the angels; that they had reached a far higher level of attainment in their worship. Paul is clear: don't let this kind of nonsense trip you up, as those who are spiritually proud try to cut you down. Some people, insisting that they are deeper, simply complicate the faith: don't let them disqualify you.

Prayer: Lord, I want to grow deeper in You, but avoid the traps that people often fall into. Keep me focused, humble and self-aware. Amen.

TUES 19 FEB

God rewards us

BIG PICTURE
Ephesians 6:1–9
Revelation 11:15–19

FOCUS:
'Serve wholeheartedly, as if you were serving the Lord, not people, because you know that the Lord will reward each one for whatever good they do, whether … slave or free.'
(Eph. 6:7–8)

IT'S time for us to think again about rewards and prizes, which feature prominently in Paul's thinking. Over the years that I've been a Christian, I can't remember too many sermons that focused on the rewards that God gives to His children, even though there are many references to the wonderful truth in Scripture. Why would we ignore the truth that a trophy day is coming (and that, in this life, as we run, God rewards us – not everything happens at the end of all things)? Perhaps we so want to emphasise that we are saved by grace alone, that we are unable to do anything to make God love us more or less, that the idea of 'earning' anything seems alien. But we're wrong; as we have already seen, the prizes God gives for service and the salvation that is freely given through Christ are quite different.

We might also hesitate to suggest that serving God is done for any other reason than simply a free response to His love for us. To think of working for rewards seems to taint that offering of our lives; we want to serve, love, give and be faithful, simply as a worshipful response to all that God has done. All that said, God, ever gracious, insists: He has rewards He wants us to enjoy. That can change our perspective when we serve hard but meet ingratitude, as we'll see.

The day is coming when not only will we see Jesus, but also He will bring His reward: 'The LORD has made proclamation to the ends of the earth: "Say to Daughter Zion, 'See, your Saviour comes! See, his reward is with him, and his recompense accompanies him'"' (Isa. 62:11).

Prayer: Strengthen me today with this truth, Lord: not only do You notice and applaud what is good, but You reward it too. Amen.

> Why would we ignore the truth that a trophy day is coming …?

WED 20 FEB

God our reward

BIG PICTURE
Genesis 15:1–21
Matthew 28:19–20

FOCUS:
'After this, the word of the LORD came to Abram in a vision: "Do not be afraid, Abram. I am your shield, your very great reward."' (Gen. 15:1)

CHRISTIANITY is not formed around the teachings of Jesus. Rather, it's formed around the living Jesus and His teachings. And we constantly need to be reminded of that, lest faith descend into our plodding along with a set of theories and ideas, forgetting that Christ is the living, risen Lord who walks with us, empowering us by His Spirit to obey Him, transforming us little by little each day. Granted, this is a relationship like no other. We can't see or touch Him, and often, we can't hear Him: it's a walk of faith. Nevertheless, it's important to remember that God Himself is our ultimate reward. Eternity will be wonderful, not because of the splendours of the heavenly state (and we have very little idea about what eternity will look like, because the Bible speaks of it in poetic language), but because we will be with Jesus and we will see Him in all His glory.

In the meantime, God gives Himself to us, immersing Himself in our lives, listening to our flawed prayers, offering guidance and direction, connecting us in relationships for purpose, and being alongside us, whether we sense His presence or not. The final promise of Jesus, prior to His ascension, was 'I will be with you, always.' The nagging questions of the disciples were not answered – but what was assured was the abiding, faithful presence of God to accompany them. Just as Abram was called to a journey both to a new land and with the Lord Himself, His shield and reward, so God gives Himself to us. He did so at the cross, and He does so, daily.

'I will be with you, always'

Prayer: Lord, thank You for the gift of Your faithful presence this day. I affirm by faith, You are with me, and always will be. Amen.

THURS 21 FEB

Blessing

BIG PICTURE
Genesis 12:1–20
Psalm 19:1–11

FOCUS:
'I will make you into a great nation, and I will bless you.' (Gen. 12:2)

WE SAW yesterday that God offered Himself to Abram as a reward; a priceless prize that was not just waiting for Abram in his eternal future, but began there and then as the faith journey unfolded: God travelling with His faithful friend. As God walks with us, we discover that the rewarding God blesses His people, in the here and now.

The psalmist celebrates the value of keeping God's commands, with the immediate rewards that come: 'By them your servant is warned; in keeping them there is great reward' (Psa. 19:11).

Abram discovered that God blessed him with a great name, a new nation, protection and financial provision. What modern, secular thinking calls 'luck', 'success' or 'breaks', the Old Testament calls 'blessing' and insists that God alone is the source of all of these good things.

Genesis is certainly a blessing book – the concept of blessing occurs 88 times in Genesis, as against 310 times total elsewhere in Scripture. This was a radical revelation to Abram: the concept of God being the blesser and rewarder. The idea of blessing is not used in classical Greek literature. For example, Zeus is not said to have bestowed any specific act of blessing on anyone. Rather he is said to have caused good luck or good fortune. But God brings with Him gifts and rewards, not just for tomorrow, in eternity, but for today.

There are incredible rewards out ahead. Let's dare to ask Him for blessing in this next 24-hour period of our lives.

Prayer: Lord, I ask, not only for blessing, but for a tenacious attitude in asking: bless me today, that I might be a blessing. Amen.

FRI 22 FEB

The Persecuted rewarded

BIG PICTURE
Matthew 5:1–12
1 Peter 3:8–22

FOCUS:
'Rejoice and be glad, because great is your reward in heaven, for in the same way they persecuted the prophets who were before you.' (Matt. 5:12)

IT WAS an inspiring and profoundly uncomfortable encounter. I had flown back to the UK to speak at a two-day conference, and was feeling just a little sorry for myself. A busy preaching schedule meant that I was sandwiching the conference between two weekends of intense teaching, in a month that had included many thousands of miles of travel. Jet lag distorts perspective, and I had completely lost sight of the privilege that is mine to meet many different people and live a life of diversity and variety; instead I was wallowing in self-pity. But I quickly snapped out of my stupidity, when I met one of the other guest speakers.

I won't go into details, but as a follower of Christ she had met opposition from the government of her nation, and they had hatched a devilishly cruel plan to try to make her relent. They took her five-year-old daughter from her, under the sham charge that, because she was a Christian, she was an unfit mother. All she had to do was deny Christ, and she'd get her daughter back. For six or seven long years, she had lived with the enforced separation. I felt utterly ashamed at my self-pity.

One day, that faithful servant of God is going to receive a reward that will not be mine. Those who have paid a high price for the gospel will receive their reward – the word means wages.

Today, may the Persecuted Church be in our prayers. Let's not forget them, but find ways to speak up through supporting the agencies that are a voice on their behalf. May their courage give us a sense of perspective.

I felt utterly ashamed at my self-pity

Prayer: I pray for those who suffer for Your name, Jesus. Bless the organisations that speak up for those who cannot speak for themselves. Amen.

NEXT ISSUE

Access All Areas MAR/APR 2013

They were His closest, most trusted companions. Peter, James and John, handpicked from the 12 disciples, were allowed exclusive access to the life and ministry of Jesus. They experienced 'for their eyes only' sights, enjoying an intimacy with Jesus that was unique and being treated to a stunning glimpse of the eternal that was designed to galvanise them in the more harrowing days. And Jesus demanded more of them, calling only them to watch and pray with Him in Gethsemane.

So who were these three, and why did Jesus invite them in when others were excluded? Next month, we'll be taking a look at the inner core – the cabinet, if you will – that Jesus formed with this famous trio. Who were they, why did they enjoy such privileges and what happened to them? Join me as we consider some truths that will enable us to walk a little more closely with Jesus ourselves.

Also available as ebook/esubscription

Obtain your copy from CWR or a Christian bookshop

23/24 FEB

Matthew 6:1–18 // Matthew 23:5–7

Just between us

There's something delicious about being viewed as better than we are. We can use prayer, fasting and giving to solicit admiration. The Pharisees were not at all subtle in their broadcasted piety; although the view held by some that they actually hired trumpeters to play a tune when they gave is unlikely to have any substance. It is far more likely that Jesus was creating a word-play with the trumpet-shaped receptacles at the Temple which were used to collect offerings. Nevertheless, they were very public in the way they practised their faith. They were fond of loud public prayers, drama when they gave, and having their faces made up especially when they were fasting. And Jesus' comment was this: they have been paid in full – the word means 'they have their receipt'. Let's beware the trap of wanting to be seen in our goodness.

One cautionary word: this is not an argument against public prayer gatherings or collective times of fasting. Jesus is not teaching that we shouldn't gather together, but is cautioning against losing prizes and rewards because of false motives.

To ponder: How do we subtly let people know that we're really spiritual?

> Let's beware the trap of wanting to be seen in our goodness

MON 25 FEB

Rewarded for loving our enemies

BIG PICTURE
Matthew 5:43–48
Luke 6:35–36

FOCUS:
'If you love those who love you, what reward will you get?' (Matt. 5:46)

ONE OF the hardest things to do is to love enemies who insist on remaining enemies. We can mistakenly think that we're called to show love that will prompt a change of heart – forgiveness, reconciliation and a new day for the relationship. It's much harder when we love, share or give – and there's no return whatsoever. The words that Jesus uses here have to do with not giving up in despair – and that's how we can feel when we are kind, only to be shown unkindness in return. Bluntly, that's often the way. Jesus speaks to that issue, calling us to love without expecting anything in return – no payback in this life. But then He assures us that this is not a wasted investment. Quite apart from the development of our own character and Christlikeness that happens when we bless when we are cursed, there's a promise of reward, of a prize from God. When we love in the face of ongoing ingratitude (and notice that the ungrateful are specifically mentioned here) then we must know that there is gratitude in the heart of God for that action. The ultimate reward might not be immediate, but it's still promised.

Incidentally, misunderstanding of verse 46 created great havoc in history, because Popes and Councils took it as teaching that Christians could never lend money with interest – and so money lending passed into the hands of the Jewish community, which in turn created resentment and contributed to raging anti-Semitism. All Scripture needs to be read and interpreted carefully.

Prayer: Help me not only to love, loving God, but to keep loving in the face of ongoing unkindness. Amen.

TUES 26 FEB

Building works tested

BIG PICTURE
1 Corinthians 3:1–23
Matthew 16:27

FOCUS:
'If what has been built survives, the builder will receive a reward.'
(1 Cor. 3:14)

I'D NEVER be much use as a builder, as my family could repeatedly testify. Just about anything I built was always destined for a certain end – it would fall over. Of course, when I first put that wardrobe together, it looked like a work of art, but constant use and the test of time revealed that I had not built well. As Paul writes especially to leaders, whose teaching will be examined and ultimately burned up or survive the test, we reaffirm that our salvation is free but our rewards come from what we have done. Jesus speaks of this as well: God does see all our works done in His name, will test them, and will reward that which survives the test. Sometimes the thought of this encourages and motivates me, and at other times it paralyses me. I am never sure about the quality of what I do, and because the heart is deceitful, I am sure that there are always mixed motives in my service.

All that said, it's wonderful to remind ourselves once more, as we draw towards the close of our journey that has been, that acts of self-sacrifice and service are not only noticed, but will be rewarded, which is especially helpful when we serve but are not appreciated – which often happens in church life. Some leaders forget to encourage, on the assumption that what is done is done for the sake of the kingdom, and so no appreciation is needed – an idea that is quite wrong.

If you find yourself in that position, then be encouraged by this: the reward ceremony is being prepared. The prizes are ahead.

Prayer: Lord, enable me to build well, in works that will not only stand the test of time, but the test of Your examination. Amen.

WED 27 FEB

A curtain call

BIG PICTURE
Hebrews 12:1–3
Psalm 25:15

FOCUS:
'Therefore, since we are surrounded by such a great cloud of witnesses ...'
(Heb. 12:1)

THE MEMORY of an epic event makes me want to take one last glance at the 'crowd of witnesses' of Hebrews 12. Among that group of witnesses who testify that God is faithful is a friend and colleague, Rob Lacey, who truly pioneered (sometimes at great personal cost) for the arts to be fully included in the life of the Church. After a brave and lengthy battle with cancer, Rob died in May 2006. I still remember travelling to see him and his wife Sandra, just weeks before he went home to be with the Lord. His faith was strong, and he wept when he spoke of his unfinished passion for the arts. No tears for his own pain, or the thought of leaving his lovely family behind, Rob grabbed hold of that for which Jesus had 'grabbed hold' of him, just like Paul the apostle, and held on tight until the end.

At his funeral service at Glenwood Church in Cardiff, there was to be a spontaneous moment of beauty as the coffin was carried down the aisle at the conclusion. Knowing that the most fitting reward for an actor is a standing ovation, someone stood to their feet and began to clap. Soon the entire congregation was on its feet, cheering and celebrating a brave fighter, a gold medal winner. Rob fought the fight, ran hard and breasted the tape. I'm sure there was not a dry eye in the place that epic day, and those who knew him still miss him. And surely this is true: Jesus was joining in the applause, clapping a 'Well done' to a good and faithful servant. Cheer others on. And remember, again, that you're cheered on too.

Prayer: Lord, when I come to the end, may I have lived a life worthy of applause from You, by Your grace. Amen.

Rob fought the fight, ran hard and breasted the tape

THURS 28 FEB

God is a sprinter

BIG PICTURE
Luke 15:11–32
Ephesians 2:11–22

FOCUS:
'But while he was still a long way off, his father saw him and was filled with compassion for him; he ran to his son, threw his arms round him and kissed him.' (Luke 15:20)

AS WE end our reflections, I thought it would be helpful for us to know that we follow a God who is also a runner. Christ is with us and goes before us as the author and pioneer of our faith, and the wonderful story of the prodigal son shows us that God is also a runner. Jesus spoke of a running father, in a culture where it was considered undignified for a man to run. The Arabic translation of Luke 15 edited out 'he ran' for over a thousand years, replacing it with 'he went'. But the father in the story becomes a sprinter, and then breathlessly commands that the party begins. Why? Because he knew that a ceremony of rejection and total banishment was likely to start any minute.

In Jesus' day, if villagers discovered that a disgraced son or daughter was trying to return home, they would gather at the edge of the village, and confront the returning prodigal with a jar of parched corn and nuts. Calling out the person's name, they would shatter the jar, declaring the relationship was irretrievably broken and the prodigal as one dead to the village.

The father ran to get there before the ceremony could begin. In the race for our hearts and lives, grace wins. Jesus' run has been a marathon: not only from the throne of heaven to the cross, but also Paul celebrates how He has come to preach to those near, and those far off. And so we run for Him and with Him, because Jesus has run out to us. And today, when we cry or call, He still comes running, whether we sense it or not, drawing near to those who draw near to Him.

And so we run for Him and with Him …

Prayer: Thank You for Your triumphant run, Lord, and that You counted me as part of the prize, for which You ran so hard. I worship You. Amen.

ORDER FORM

LED J/F 13

5 EASY WAYS TO ORDER:

1. Phone in your credit card order: **01252 784710** (Mon-Fri, 9.30am - 5pm)
2. Visit our Online Store at **www.cwr.org.uk/store**
3. Send this form together with your payment to:
   CWR, Waverley Abbey House, Waverley Lane, Farnham, Surrey GU9 8EP
4. Visit a Christian bookshop
5. For Australia and New Zealand visit KI Entertainment at **www.cwr4u.net.au**

For a list of our National Distributors, who supply countries outside of the UK, visit www.cwr.org.uk/distributors

YOUR DETAILS (REQUIRED FOR ORDERS AND DONATIONS)

Name:	CWR ID No. (if known):
Home Address:	
	Postcode:
Telephone No. (for queries):	Email:

PUBLICATIONS

TITLE	QTY	PRICE	TOTAL
		Total publications	

All CWR adult Bible-reading notes are also available in ebook and email subscription format.
Visit www.cwr.org.uk for further information.

UK p&p: up to £24.99 = **£2.99**; £25.00 and over = **FREE**

Elsewhere p&p: up to £10 = **£4.95**; £10.01 - £50 = **£6.95**; £50.01 - £99.99 = **£10**; £100 and over = **£30**

Total publications and p&p A | |

Please allow 14 days for delivery

SUBSCRIPTIONS* (NON DIRECT DEBIT)

	QTY	PRICE (INCLUDING P&P)			TOTAL
		UK	Europe	Elsewhere	
Every Day with Jesus (1yr, 6 issues)		£15.95	£19.95	Please contact nearest National Distributor or CWR direct	
Large Print *Every Day with Jesus* (1yr, 6 issues)		£15.95	£19.95		
Inspiring Women Every Day (1yr, 6 issues)		£15.95	£19.95		
Life Every Day (Jeff Lucas) (1yr, 6 issues)		£15.95	£19.95		
Cover to Cover Every Day (1yr, 6 issues)		£15.95	£19.95		
Mettle: 14-18s (1yr, 3 issues)		£14.50	£16.60		
YP's: 11-15s (1yr, 6 issues)		£15.95	£19.95		
Topz: 7-11s (1yr, 6 issues)		£15.95	£19.95		
Total Subscriptions (Subscription prices already include postage and packing) **B**					

Please circle which bimonthly issue you would like your subscription to commence from:

JAN/FEB MAR/APR MAY/JUN JUL/AUG SEP/OCT NOV/DEC

* Only use this section for subscriptions paid for by credit/debit card or cheque. For Direct Debit subscriptions see overleaf.

CONTINUED OVERLEAF >>

« SEE PREVIOUS PAGE FOR START OF ORDER FORM

PAYMENT DETAILS

☐ I enclose a cheque/PO made payable to CWR for the amount of: £ _____

☐ Please charge my credit/debit card.

Cardholder's name (in BLOCK CAPITALS) _____

Card No. [ ][ ][ ][ ][ ][ ][ ][ ][ ][ ][ ][ ][ ][ ][ ][ ]

Expires end [ ][ ][ ]   Security Code [ ][ ][ ]

GIFT TO CWR

☐ Please send me an acknowledgement of my gift   **C** [ ]

giftaid it

I am a UK taxpayer and want CWR to reclaim the tax on all my donations for the four years prior to this year **and on** all donations I make from the date of this Gift Aid declaration until further notice.*

Taxpayer's Full Name (please use BLOCK CAPITALS) _____

Signature _____ **Date** _____

*I understand I must pay an amount of Income/Capital Gains Tax at least equal to the tax the charity reclaims in the tax year.

GRAND TOTAL (Total of A, B, & C) [ ]

SUBSCRIPTIONS BY DIRECT DEBIT (UK BANK ACCOUNT HOLDERS ONLY)

Subscriptions cost £15.95 (except *Mettle*: £14.50) for one year for delivery within the UK. Please tick relevant boxes and fill in the form be

☐ *Every Day with Jesus* (1yr, 6 issues)
☐ Large Print *Every Day with Jesus* (1yr, 6 issues)
☐ *Inspiring Women Every Day* (1yr, 6 issues)
☐ *Life Every Day* (Jeff Lucas) (1yr, 6 issues)
☐ *Cover to Cover Every Day* (1yr, 6 issues)
☐ *Mettle*: 14-18s (1yr, 3 issues)
☐ *YP's*: 11-15s (1yr, 6 issues)
☐ *Topz*: 7-11s (1yr, 6 issues)

Issue to commence fr
☐ Jan/Feb ☐ Jul/Aug
☐ Mar/Apr ☐ Sep/Oct
☐ May/Jun ☐ Nov/Dec

CWR

Instruction to your Bank or Building Society to pay by Direct Debit

DIRECT Debit

Please fill in the form and send to: CWR, Waverley Abbey House, Waverley Lane, Farnham, Surrey GU9 8EP

Name and full postal address of your Bank or Building Society

To: The Manager _____ Bank/Building Society

Address _____

Postcode _____

Name(s) of Account Holder(s)

Branch Sort Code [ ][ ] [ ][ ] [ ][ ]

Bank/Building Society account number [ ][ ][ ][ ][ ][ ][ ][ ]

Originator's Identification Number

| 4 | 2 | 0 | 4 | 8 | 7 |

Reference [ ][ ][ ][ ][ ][ ][ ][ ][ ][ ]

Instruction to your Bank or Building Society

Please pay CWR Direct Debits from the account detailed in this Instruction sub to the safeguards assured by the Direct Debit Guarantee.

I understand that this Instruction may remain with CWR and, if so, details will be passed electronically to my Bank/Building Society.

Signature(s) _____

Date _____

Banks and Building Societies may not accept Direct Debit Instructions for some types of account